The Poetry of Flowers

Also by Lost Tower Publications

Poetry

Poems from the Witching Hour
Hope Springs a Turtle
Dog Days: A Celebration of Dogs
The Gift of a Rose
The Black Rose of Winter
Bridge of Fates
Purrfect Poetry
Eastern Voices
Journeys Along the Silk Road
Greek Fire
And the Tail Wagged On...
Temptation
Shout It Out!

The Poetry of Flowers

Lost Tower Publications asserts its copyright over this book as an anthology.

However, Lost Tower Publications does not have copyright for the individual poems printed herein.

Each contributor has kindly agreed to have their work published by Lost Tower Publications within this anthology.

The copyright of any of the poems published within remains the copyright of the authors.

The copyright of any of the photographs published within remains the copyright of the photographers.

This collection is published by Lost Tower Publications.

LTP publish a wide range of poetry and fiction titles and are renowned for passion, quality and individuality.

Lost Tower Publications

The Poetry of Flowers

The Poetry of Flowers

Contents

Introduction	Duncan Morrish	10-14
The Poems	The Poets	Pages
haiku blossoms	Mary Bone	15-17
	Priya Patel	
	P.J. Reed	
	Elisavietta Ritchie	
	Heidi Willson	
Lateness	Sheikha A.	18
Rojo Rose Love	Kimmy Alan	19
An Undying Love	Jasmine Allen	20
Yoni	Dr Nicole Antoine	21
Serendipity and Wit	Donna Barkman	22
Nasturtiums and Moonlight	Lana Bella	23
Vibrant Spring	Mary Bone	24
Collinsia Verna	Debbi Brody	25
Secret Flowers	Lissie Bull	26
Funeral Flowers	Wanda Morrow Clevenger	27
Flourishes Under the Eyelids	Mariela Cordero	28
Dandelion Time	Philip Dodd	29
Thunder Lily	Fathima E.V.	30
Blue Daisy	Kaitlyn Fox	31
Flowers: Colours and Beauty Never Say Goodbye	Mark Frank	32
Surreal Mind Garden	Cleveland W. Gibson	33-34
a petal's perspective	Ingrid Gjelsvik	35
Tulip - the essence of innocence	Norbert Gora	36

The Amaranth	Kristyl Gravina	37
Ode to the Flower	Carol Lynn Grellas	38-39
A Warm Welcome	Eric Harvey	40
Blossoms Bursting	Debbie Johnson	41
Redwood Flower	Wendy Joseph	42
Daisy	Tim Kahl	43
Plant Them for Me!	Kaikasi V.S.	44-45
A Sonnet for Van Gogh	Linda Kraus	46
Big Root	Richard Krawiec	47
Spring in the Garden	Alicja Kuberska	48
Sunflower	Alicja Kuberska	49
Wil-o'-the-Wisp	John Lambremont Sr.	50
A Crocus Blooms	Joan Leotta	51
The Fate of a Beautiful Flower	Indunil Madhusankha	52
Wintry Bouquet	Joan McNerney	53
Prunus Blossom Bottle	Ian Mole	54
Flowers for My Love	Duncan Morrish	55
Chuppah	Ceri Naz	56
God	Ashraf V. Nediyanad	57
Sunflowers	Bozena Helena Mazur-Nowak	58
A Dewy Rosebud	Afzal Nusker	59
Nature's Gem	Amy S. Pacini	60
Orchid	Grace Pasco	61-63
Flower Picker	Akshaya Pawaskar	64
Floricultural Traditions: Warning	Elisavietta Ritchie	65
Lilacs	Elisavietta Ritchie	66
Pumpkin Flowers	Elspeth C. Ritchie	67-68
Heart-flower	Bethany Rivers	69
Led by the Nose	Vincent Van Ross	70

Vernal Observance	Ceò Ruaírc	71
Fortuna's Garden	Miriam Sagan	72
Morning Delight	Neethu Sasikumar	73
Introduction to Photographs of Flowers	Don Schaeffer	74
Adornment	Sunil Sharma	75
Where They Belonged	Eleanor Sivins	76
Sunrise Altar	Dennis Trujillo	77
Flower Garden and Mind	Bhisma Upreti	78
Manet: Peonies in a Vase	Sylvia Riojas Vaughn	79
Stars in My Garden	Sylvia Riojas Vaughn	80
Scent of a Rose	Lita Verella	81
Pheromones	Marion de Vos	82
Ikebana	John Ward	83
Survivor	Robert West	84
Withered Rose	Heidi Willson	85
Lady Convolvulus	Abigail Wyatt	86
Valerian	Abigail Wyatt	87

Acknowledgments	89
Art Work	90
Bibliography	91
Biography of Poets	92-106

The Poetry of Flowers

Introduction

The Poetry of Flowers anthology is a worldwide appreciation of the beauty and mystique of the humble flower and garden. Poets from America, Canada, England, Holland, India, Malta, Nepal, Norway, Pakistan, the Philippines, Poland, South Africa, Sri Lanka, and Venezuela have all offered their admiration, displaying a wide range of interpretation in their love, affection and relationships with the world of flora.

Flowers are well known to have many different symbolisms – the red rose is often connoted with stories of love, whilst the red of the poppy offers hope and prosperity in light of death. In many cultures, flowers such as the lily are used to symbolise life and resurrection, associating with the sun; in fact, most, if not all flowers will have meaning to someone, somewhere – be it a cultural association, or a personal story.

It appears to be that, for as long as humans have reaped and sowed the land, flowers have played an important role for us. As the human race, our brain is built in such a way that beauty is unavoidably admired; a fact that has led us to ascribe so much meaning to the flowers we see beauty in.

In terms of the history of the flower, recently discovered evidence from a team led by researcher Dani Nadel has led us to believe that flowers were being domesticated as early as 5000 years ago, as decorations. This team also discovered a multitude of graves from over 13,500 years ago with beds made from flowers, for the dead. [3]
This highlighted the suggestions from evolutionary psychology that even all those years ago, flowers elicited positive the same emotional responses, which can be seen throughout cultural development of the human race. [1]

Due to the beauty of flowers, the Ancient Egyptians arrived at the idea they were created specifically for the gods. It is for this reason that many temples were surrounded by gardens, and adorned with flowers; these flowers were likely to have had additional religious meaning ascribed to them as each one would be associated with a certain god or goddess. [2]

Perhaps the most famous gardens in the world however, are the potentially mythical hanging gardens of Babylon, one of the seven wonders of the ancient world. It is claimed that 6th century BC King Nebuchadnezzar built them out of love for his wife, Queen Amytis. According to the word of 'Quintus Curtius Rufus,' a writer in the 1st century AD, '[t]radition has it that it is the work of a Syrian king who ruled from Babylon. He built it out of love for his wife who missed the flowers, woods and forests in this flat country and persuaded her husband to imitate nature's beauty with a structure of this kind'. [4] The extravagance of such a gesture is a clear indication of how much the beauty of the garden can influence an individual's happiness – that these plants that have no apparent function can be enough to fill a queen with joy, alongside the reminders of home.

It is not just King Nebuchadnezzar who used flowers for romantic purposes however – this is a trend that has carried through to the modern era. We see these tokens of love across all stages of companionship; perhaps a carefully, handpicked rose on a first date, to a beautiful bouquet of a bride on her wedding day, the significance and symbolism is still apparent.

The relationship between love and flowers is one often explored in the arts, with pieces such as Van Gogh's *Twelve Sunflowers in a Vase*. The versatility of both literal and metaphorical meaning of the flower makes them a frequent candidate within the arts – at a base level, the description, or painting of a floral scene can take beauty from its literal image – but read deeper into the words, or delve further into the inspirations for a painting and the image can take on meaning deeper than first thought. It has been surmised that in this case, the sunflower represents happiness, warmth and love. Van Gogh, may have been aiming to put to the fore the love that was seemingly hidden in his heart; a love we hear little to nothing about from the unusual character.

The Poetry of Flowers

The Poetry of Flowers

Flowers themselves are also common stimuli within the arts; with Monet's *Blue Water Lilies* a prime example of their use in the 20th century, whilst Banksy's Rage, *Flower Thrower* an example in the modern era. As aforementioned, the versatility of a flower's meaning lends itself to becoming a widely used focus in art.

In Monet's piece, it is simply said that he always enjoyed the beauty of the lilies he held in his garden, so much so that he decided to paint them; Banksy, on the other hand, prescribes hidden meaning to his flowers; in this image, a protester is seen in the process of throwing a vase of flowers, an oxymoronic image on the surface.
No one is sure exactly what the painting's message was, but based on its location and the time of creation (in Jerusalem after protests at a gay pride rally by anti-gay individuals) the flowers have often been seen as a symbol of the gay community – this is furthered by the fact that the flowers are the only colourful parts of the painting; the rainbow being a symbol of the community. Even by comparing these two pieces, we see the vast difference of meaning a flower can take on, with their importance in the art world paramount.

In the realms of literature, there is clear abundancy in the use of floral language – the most obvious literary example, William Shakespeare, often referred to flowers to evoke vivid imagery in his audience's mind, such as in '*A Midsummer Night's Dream*;' Oberon, King of the Fairies, converses with his messenger, Puck, about where Queen Titania is sleeping: he refers to 'oxlips,' 'nodding violets,' 'woodbine,' 'musk-roses' and 'eglantine' in only one line. [5]

In poetry, it is of course also a prominent feature, with many inspirational, famous poets taking the flower as their muse. Again, using a hugely prominent example in William Wordsworth, we see that flowers take pride of place in some of his most famous quotes. For example, by looking at his 'Ode: Intimations of Immortality' we can take the quote 'that though

the radiance which was once so bright be now forever taken from my sight. Though nothing can bring back the hour of splendour in the grass, glory in the flower. We will grieve not, rather find strength in what remains behind.' [6]
Emily Dickinson, the American poetess, was particularly fond of flowers; according to Judith Farr's *'The Gardens of Emily Dickinson'* over a third of her poems "allude with passionate intensity to her favourite wildflowers, to traditional blooms like the daisy or gentian, and to the exotic gardenias and jasmines of her conservatory."[7]

Along with these famous poets of the past, our poets in this anthology see the meaning deep beyond the physical flower. There are some incredible insights into this often explored world that will leave you seeing the simple flower as an intricate sculpture of beauty, full of distinct and hidden meaning. In this anthology, Elspeth C. Ritchie's 'Pumpkin Flowers' is a perfect blend of imagery from description, paired with intelligent, emotional metaphor. Mark Frank's 'Flowers: Colour and Beauty Never Say Goodbye' focuses purely on the beauty of the flower, with his use of imagery creating a clear, vivid picture to the reader – it is almost as if he has painted a picture of the scene with his words.

This anthology has been created to celebrate the beauty that we see in front of us – perhaps in this modern era, the exquisite nature of the flower has been overlooked by the masses. By celebrating both the beauty and the message attributed to flowers, we may go some way to reinstating the appreciation that the flower should receive; an appreciation that the poets in our anthology clearly hold very close.

by Duncan Morrish 2016

Haiku Blossoms

colourful flowers
beautiful visions to see
life's fragrant moments.
Mary Bone

cool breezes whisper
softly to the sleeping earth
dandelion yawns
P.J. Reed

ants travel up stem
attracted to sweet nectar
insect army helps
Heidi Willson

petals wilt with change
still a beauty untainted
breathlessly they fall
Priya Patel

the august sorrows
crumbling cream rose petals fall
stolen by the breeze
P.J. Reed

The Poetry of Flowers

The Poetry of Flowers

if one dandelion
is the one bloom in your yard
cherish dandelions
Elisavietta Ritchie

whispers of summer
ferns uncurl and leaves unwrap
bathing in the sun
P.J. Reed

green fresh wrapped petals
burst through tired hedgerows bank
impetuous youth
P.J. Reed

poor yellow flower
stands tall in her concrete crack
is this poverty
P.J. Reed

Sheikha A.
Lateness

We grew up with paper flowers,
pale pink scentless petals springing
from real leaves; they were the only

flowers we knew, hanging from
thornless stems like perfection
known only by the grains of its

dark brown artificial soil; the naming
sensibilities for labelling all things
of tangible properties didn't meddle

with our sights that we bothered to fill
with just its beauty; we never knew
of how well a rose could grow from

the roots of deserts, for we lived
in a world where berries were picked
from plant enclosures, and in our

wildest moments we would declare
them poisoned to live the thrills of
foliage-familiar gardens of flowers

that grew in brighter shades
than our glossy textbook images;
and somewhere the auburn winds

would hustle woodpeckers from
eating their wood, and rainbow-
rains would paint orchids on easels

of belated springs.

from a Pakistani garden

Kimmy Alan
Rojo Rose Love

You cannot grow roses
And not expect to bleed
Every lover of roses knows this

Pain sates their need
Ask any rose gardener
Blood meal is their feed

True love will also cause you pain
For someday one lover will die
And the other will remain

For Love and Roses
Are one and the same
Pain and suffering
Is part of the game

from an American garden

Jasmine Allen
An Undying Love

Last night I dreamed of
azure forget-me-nots,
showering lustrously from the heavens,
And as they fell towards me,
stars fell too,
Yet the radiance emitted by the angelic little flowers,
did not die.

from an American garden

Dr Nicole Antoine
Yoni

Petals peel and part
in full bloom
while careful fingers trace

Translucent veins that swell, blush
atop palms, heated and damp
from dew-kissed curves

And like cream churned, soft and silken
she unfolds, giving in to touch
Shakti goddess fulfilled, sated

As fragrant beads scent tepid air
blessing the broken things
scattered and sacred

Beneath cooled earth
she rises, beautifully poised
sublime and feminine

Igniting senses
relishing Nature's
life flower

from an American garden

Donna Barkman
Serendipity and Wit

- after An Artist [Begins Her Life's Work] at 72.
Molly Peacock, subtitle for *The Paper Garden*

The happenstance of a few fallen petals, geranium red –
heeded by the keen eye of Mrs. Mary Delany, who then,
with initiative and acumen, snipped identical paper shapes
of a matching shade, layering them as the flower itself had
done.

Magnolia followed, along with lobelia, nodding thistle,
damask rose, winter cherry, opium poppy, bloodroot,
all stunning in their verisimilitude of contour and hue: saffron,
scarlet, vermilion, cerise, turquoise, ivory, indigo, gold.

Each mosaic she produced – near one thousand --
was botanically correct, leaf-, stem-, and petal-perfect,
frank in its display of a blossom's sexuality: pistils
and stamens aroused in 18th century Georgian England.

May Mrs. Delany's lucky petals fall again
in metaphoric splendour before my eager eyes
awakening me to spit and fire with sensuality of word
and fearlessness of deed at whatever age I shall begin.

from an American garden

Lana Bella
Nasturtiums and Moonlight

as I stared
into the immediate world,
dimness clamoured
toward the unlit porch light
then skyward,
in pursuit of phosphorous compound,

somewhere behind me,
shadows drank in the blue beach chairs
and the brush of nasturtium vines
over my back,

spotted with burst of flames
of the rising moon,
a spiral of yellow red from the nasturtiums
yawned out to the frost,
moved in the rawness of my open hands,

beneath the blooms,
the edges of the moon softened, leaving halos
upon the earth in
monochromatic white,

I reached up
and turned on the porch light,
the moon glowed as if in feverish prayer,
its gold fingertips stretched across
the nasturtiums
like tine fork scraped over butter--

from an American garden

Mary Bone
Vibrant Spring

Clouds dispersed
Raindrops splattered.
Little seed drank
and sprouted out.
Spring welcomed
this new arrival.
Flowers held promise
of a vibrant spring.

from an American garden

Debbi Brody
Collinsia Verna

Before the upgrade, the chosen path, the project,
the innovation, the design,
before making, beading, quilting, thatching,
before guilt, sorrow, pain, change, joy, reason, recollection
before Eros, Loki, Ra, Baal, Lilith and Thor
there grew and grows still, blue-eyed-Mary.

Her third name, Innocence, flows from two lips,
bottom petals blue, topped by pure white. Simple
to write of innocence lost, the apex of a prior story,
a challenge to pen a tale of enduring innocence,
except in flowers, so complete millenniums
later they give air, food, paroxysm of blood.

They know not what they created unacquainted
with the not yet invented devil, they green
into eternity... unless the evil they accidentally birthed
should fry or freeze their only world.

Innocence blossoms bi-coloured, a slip of worm inside.

from an American garden

Lissie Bull
Secret Flowers

a sensual moment
in the summer breeze
sweet alluring scent
wafting through the trees

with thin slender stems
swaying all together
they raise their heads tall
making most of the weather

petals tilted to the sun
in the warm afternoon light
showing off their beauty
in this secluded site

from an English garden

Wanda Morrow Clevenger
Funeral Flowers

For a great while I fancied gladiola
for my coffin lid, this simple single
palate predominate those few viewings
before I'd lived long enough to note
a shift in funeral finery

and stubbornly colour biased,
I hated yellow
clear back to crayons
and briefly pink and never
planted gladiola that remind
of funerals or marigold—orange
more officious than yellow.

Less biased with age I find
myself at last enamoured
with every bloom of every colour.
Even a black rose glistens
with the sun.

So send me off on
a neon carpet of
purple and orange
and red. Throw in some
yellow just for grins.

from an American garden

Mariela Cordero
Flourishes Under the Eyelids

Everything is impermanent
but the moment that announces
flowering
almond
It is the breath of a weightless
truce.

The fullness of these petals
swaying in the wind
will remain
under the closed eyelids.

And it will be born of silence
Ripped
for the beauty
a forest of almond trees
eternal
that will fill the heart.

from a Venezuelan garden

Philip Dodd
Dandelion Time

Let me take time to discuss the dandelion.
From my kitchen window I saw it, just now.
All by itself it grows in my back garden,
on the edge of the lawn I have yet to mow this year,
between the bench, the bins and the fence.
Maybe, I thought, it only sprouted this afternoon.
Certainly, I did not notice it there, yesterday.
Let me consider what it means to me.
Firstly, it is a welcome sign of spring.
If summer is bold, spring is shy,
showing itself in small ways,
like a lone dandelion.
I went outside, to look at it, closely.
Took two photographs of it,
which is unusual for me, odd.
Looked to me in the grass like a yellow sun,
reflected on a green sea from a green sky.
No, not a weed to me, as it would be
to keen gardeners, as they are called, dismissed as such
by them, uprooted and dumped on a waste heap,
for only flowers they plant themselves from seed bags
have beauty in their eyes, but what it is, a wild flower,
like the bluebell, the snowdrop.
When the ground is dry and I mow the grass,
the dandelion will remain, like a sun beam in a green glass.
Dandelion is from the French *dent-de-lion*,
which means lion's tooth, I read.
How they came by that, I do not know.
Does not make me think of a lion or a tooth.
Sunshine, yes, as I have said.

from an English garden

Fathima E.V.
Thunder Lily

Startled by the rumble
of wild rainy nights
when clouds kiss
lightning rushes down
the lily blooms in alarm, crimson.

In testimony of passionate nights
Subterranean meetings, the tiny flowers
stand in unison, a fiery sphere of spikes
their perfect pinball displayed
straining on a shamelessly long stalk.

from an Indian garden

Kaitlyn Fox
Blue Daisy

Blue daisy with petals of the sea,
do not let others tell you who to be.
Ignore the pink flowers and yellow ones too;
because of your bright colour, I'd pick you.

Others will try to paint away the colour you grew,
but never let them phase your beautiful blue.
They'll tell you you're wrong and to die away,
but it's people like me who wish you would stay.

Blue daisy with petals of the sky,
do not let them make your colours go dry.
They will tear each petal off 'til what's left of you is none;
stand proud, you'd regret it if they won.

Often you ask, 'Why me?'
It's because it is you they want to be.
They know you are a favourite to the crowd,
so don't silence your colours - Let them be loud!

Blue daisy with petals of the sea,
do not let others tell you who to be.
Ignore the pink flowers and yellow ones too;
because of your bright colour, I'd pick you.

from an American garden

Mark Frank
Flowers: Colour and Beauty Never Say Goodbye

Glorious splendour prostrated under a delightful green tree
The flowers of tomorrow lift the sky
Colour and beauty never say goodbye
A magnificent shade of purple reflects royalty
It burns with happiness under a watchful sky

The composition of the columbine is on time
Standing in beauty with heads bowed in worship
The collective variance embraces the kingship of nature
The flowers of tomorrow lift the sky
Colour and beauty never say goodbye
It burns with happiness under a watchful sky

Rooted in the ground their neighbours' faces are blue
With an elegant charm the Siberian iris spreads its wings
Birds and insects often sing around them displaying their intricate design
No human face can decline the value of flowers
The power of its composition is embedded in the soul of man

The flowers of tomorrow lift the sky
Colour and beauty never say goodbye
It burns with happiness under a watchful sky
Flowers reflect the royalty of man

from a South African garden

Cleveland W. Gibson
Surreal Mind Garden

Flowers grow within me:
quite special in my mind.
I nurture them, love them,
watching how they unwind.

Better than other ones,
these three flowers of mine,
excite, thrill, how I feel,
no need for drugs, or wine.

I mean the humble rose,
Queen of artistic grace,
her red petals capture me
spellbound, held in my place.

Oh rose! Go on and on,
like rhythms in a song,
symbolic too in looks.
Quiet. Faint echo of a gong.

Then cup shaped tulip,
her colours going wild,
blue, yellow, red, such shades,
delight any little child.

Dutch loved the tulip,
they made it all their own.
Now see inside my mind
her beauty has a home.

Then last but first perhaps,
the snowdrop from the sky,
a message from the stars,
God, and Angels on high,

The Poetry of Flowers

She tells me winter's gone,
the snow will vanish too,
quite soon the sky will change
from black to grey, to blue.

Surreal flowers thrive,
perfect beauty each day,
in my surreal-mind garden.
What more can a man say?

from an English garden

Ingrid Gjelsvik
a petal's perspective

deserted
ready and colourful
from floating touch
of silky specks

as the butterfly takes off

from a Norwegian garden

Norbert Gora
Tulip – the essence of innocence

Velvet princess sways in the wind,
with every nod more beautiful,
shines bathed in the golden glow of the sun,
spreads her charm, its power pierces the thick clouds.

Those petals electrify the senses,
colour palette seduces like a lover,
catches the eye, enslaves as whispers
before the rapture of love.

Once it looks like a burning flame,
once is mild like amaranth robe,
each gust of wind reveals its new face,
changes united with stem forever.

Velvet princess waves against a blue sky,
an image of floral miracle, indescribable,
pride dancing with sensuality,
woven into poetic journeys.

from a Polish garden

Kristyl Gravina
The Amaranth

The sound of buzzing bees
on rainbow coloured petals
which dotted meadows everywhere
When the Spring began

The English daisies gathered all around
Like little children at a playground

The daffodils dazzling scent arose
to conquer beings through their nose

Pink roses stood so elegantly
their beauty to none compared

But when the Spring was over
only the Amaranth stood there

A spot of crimson amongst the withering
Like the last drop of blood
from a dying heart
True to its name
love-lies-bleeding

from a Maltese garden

Carol Lynn Grellas
Ode to the Flower

Chrysanthemum with petals sweetly clustered
how you dance on windy days, like children
welcoming the breeze of spring, yet flustered

when a waft of air undoes the aura
though you bend with all the grace of summer
nearing fall in awe, oh fragrant flora.

Mimosa, you're a tree so ever shy
with leaves too sensitive; we ought naught touch
naivety a virtue. Virgin beauties to the passerby

I shall admire every pinkish sphere
allowing distance for your timid blush
but still I find your fearful ways most dear

coquettish as a girlish- bloom for all to fawn
perhaps you peek through secret clouds at dawn

Bright daffodil with upturned trumpet bell
where angels hearken for your sunlit notes
a trail of bees make love to you, the swell

of yellowness that bleeds from petal tips
how glorious to hold you in my hand
behold the softness of each bloom that slips

along my fingers. How I'd love to wear
your gloried shade all woven deep with ribbons
ornaments of you through washed and braided hair

a golden chord that beckons Heaven's grass
for one who grows within the blades of green
carefree as though a life will never pass

The Poetry of Flowers

if I could live like you instead of me
so gratified with just the love from every bee

The lily, purist thing I've ever seen
a fleur-de-lis extraordinaire so pale
your reign as regal as a country's queen

even so a helplessness prevails sometimes
because you are among the blessed group
with cemeteries calling you. God chimes

his church bells from Cathedrals in the sky
to those who find you comforting you go
when death has made a home for you to lie

above their dwelling as they rest alone
you keep them company dressed up in white
perfume the air with ecstasy-cologne

The birds create an aria around
your sacred place where children come and wait-
and now I'll lie my tired body down

that I may hear the sleeping of the dead
and place your bloom atop each grassy bed.

from an American garden

Eric Harvey
A Warm Welcome

Hello dear friends and welcome all.
I hope my garden will enthral,
Allow me...in my seventieth year,
To show the thing I hold most dear.

Just through the trellised concave gate,
A world of shrubs and flowers wait,
White summer house that stands serene,
Among the foliage so green.

Down brick path lay 'neath hydrangeas,
That carry scent to passing strangers,
When stepping on the chamomile,
Sweet smell of apples leaves a smile.

The ox-eye daisies straight ahead,
Alongside dahlias in their bed,
Blue lavender emits perfume,
Beneath the golden rods in bloom.

It's here in this sequestered place,
In God's own garden, full of grace,
I took her hand...fell to one knee,
And asked my love to marry me.

'Twas fifty years ago today,
And one year since she passed away,
I now sit here in transience,
In our garden of remembrance.

from an English garden

Debbie Johnson
Blossoms Bursting

Beautiful blossoms bursting
Flower garden grown with love
Blooms pretty purple foxglove
My secret place for resting

All through the day I'm sitting
Dreaming peaceful as a dove
Beautiful blossoms bursting
Flower garden grown with love

Afternoons spent enjoying
Such a peaceful, pretty cove
My veritable treasure trove
I watch anticipating
Beautiful blossoms bursting
Flower garden grown with love

from an American garden

Wendy Joseph
Redwood Flower

At the base of a giant redwood grows
A half hidden, leaf shaded blossom
Splintered amethyst on white
And on its clusters of rough edged leaves
A pine needle leans precariously
Trembling in the half risen breeze
Ready to fall, but it stays
At angles to its bashful prop

The morning grows, the whisper blows
The half touching needle, wavering, holds
Aslant the stem, an awkward rest
For a spindle of the tree

A quivered arrow, unslung
Needless and almost falling
But it stays; it stays
Upon the shag edged, ragged leaf
Gracing the base of a redwood

from an American garden

Tim Kahl
Daisy

The care of the daisy begins
with a modest glance at its stem
a little water that believes
and the sun offering its comic head

I say this only because each day ends
with a beautiful view:
wind billowing through grass gone to seed
a night cloud turning darker overhead
that no one has written a story for yet

The daisy turns to the mirror in its head
that bears witness to its former self
the only thing it reveals is
how slowly the soil moves

Then the rain drives the daisy to submit
The avid sun forces it into foetal position
I saw how cruel the seasons are to you
Let me lie down beside you in this field

The others can see we are both depressed
Daisy, let me guess just how you feel
I ask you openly with only these eyes

from an American garden

Kaikasi V.S.
Plant Them for Me!

Charming nights
Cool, fragrant breeze
An eternal quest for an ideal gift
Kept me wide awake and I
Like a mad traveller ---
Searched every garden
searching for that perfect flower...
That special bloom of the dawn
The harbinger of spring
The hope of summer
The anguish of autumn
The dirge of winter
I brought her a bunch of white roses
Spotless as her bosom
She held it with her hands ---
Her eyes at the bleeding thorns
Is she consoling them? I wondered
I stood amidst a poppy field
Love as a chasm engulfed me!!
Dazed in an army of red volunteers
I picked the luscious ones for her ... My hands
Trembling with anxiety ... She smiled
She held them to her heart!!
Tears rolled down her cheeks
You robbed the field ...
This time I made no choices
Gathered a whole bunch of tulips
Pink, white, red...
She dropped the bouquet ... The flowers scattered
She held my hand, took me to a garden,
Multitude of fragrant thoughts
Colours of rainbow
I reached for a red rose and her hands stopped me!!!
If you love me!!! Plant them for me!!
Plant them for me!!!
Let the flowers bloom!!!

The Poetry of Flowers

Bloom everywhere
This is what a girl longs for ----
'Plant them for me!!! Will you?'

from an Indian garden

Linda Kraus

A Sonnet for Van Gogh

Vincent snatched the sun from the heavens,
brilliantly electrifying his paintings.
Suddenly it was transfigured as a flower
spilling its seeds on to the blank canvas.
He had long admired the sunflowers
growing on the slopes of Montmartre.
They radiated an intense yellow pigment
as their orbs reflected transient light.
Seven times he painted his chosen totem,
the only flower he claimed as his own,
symbolic of his unthinkable fall from grace –
the cessation of his friendship with Gauguin.

The piercing rays of its florets seduce us –
a fitting paean to the majesty of Vincent's sun.

from an American garden

Richard Krawiec
Big Root

Some pretty up this weed,
call it moonflower,
sacred datura, morning glory.
When I was a boy of twelve,
chaffed and galled by the humid steam
of Louisiana Augusts, I bent low to rip them
from the rows of soybeans, hoe deep with fingers
so small I could barely scrape out the tubers,
I cursed it by its true name – Big Root. Cursed
my place here, in the drought-splintered fields
yanking from the ground this dangerous beauty,

beloved by the people cooling behind shaded windows
in the distant white house I would never know.

Now, slowly stooping against back muscles
spasming from a lifetime rooted to bending
over rows and weeds, ripping out flowers
to save handfuls of beans, seeds, in fields and out,
I cup the air knowing this is all that's left me,
all I can touch, the only beauty which lasts,
a flower I never beheld curling to fade.

from an American garden

Alicja Kuberska
Spring in the Garden

Air smells of lilac in the May evening.
The bunches of white and blue flowers bloom.
The lilies of the valley rise above the leaves
And overshadow the modest beauty of daisies.
The inconspicuous violets crouched close to the ground.
Small flowers delight with exquisite fragrance.
Jasmine bushes join this symphony of smells.

The warm wind wafts down the petals of flowering trees.
It paints tiny, white specks on the green grass.
Nature creates another moving picture
And invites us to observe life awakened.
We sit on the terrace and look with wonder as
Magnolias toast the health of bees and singing birds.

We again find the joy of existence.
You take my hand and put it on your heart.
I feel its beating - no need to say anything.
I look at you and my smile says - I know everything

from a Polish garden

Alicja Kuberska
Sunflower

Grown slender,
tall and handsome
on the strong green stalk,
reaching up to the sky
like the Greek statue of Atlas,
holding the clouds heavy
with rain.

In love with the gold of sun's rays,
reflected in his crown of petals,
he stood straight,
face turned up and smiling.

Late autumn the sun faded pale
and so did his love.
The Sunflower's heavy head
turned down.
Black seeds fell to the ground
like bitter tears...

from a Polish garden

John Lambremont Sr
Will o'-the-Wisp

The sprouting spring lawn,
a micro-cosmos of meadow,
is a green pond awash
in quick-growing grasses
and flowering herbage;
dandelions, buttercups,
and clumps of clover abound;
tiny white flowers atop long stems
hover above in observance;
a lone thistle in thorny crown
stands taller than all, bristling
in its dare to be chopped
and trimmed for its tasty stalk,
at the risk of the pricking of fingers.

The soft south breeze puts all in sway,
drawing a gaze with the seduction
of simplicity, transfixing the viewer
in a temporary floral rapture as deep
and mesmerizing as the four-
hour fixation of the junkie
with his foot while on a nod.

The events of the day
pull the viewer away,
and as he mounts his ride,
he thinks it a shame, in a way,
to mow it all down,
but he knows what must be done,
over and over,
until winter comes.

from an American garden

Joan Leotta
A Crocus Blooms

Petals pressed, close
in nightly prayer,
trying to stay warm.
spring's warming dawn
gently wakens each
kissing petals with dew
calling crocus to
spread its arms,
open to praise
the new, bright day.

from an American garden

Indunil Madhsankha
The Fate of a Beautiful Flower

In a glamorous morning,
a gorgeous flower had blossomed
with a ferocious texture of vermillion glow
Glinting dews on feathery petals
bursting in brilliance like sequins
with its soothing velvet touch
Swarms of bees buzzing around
for hunting and gathering pollen
mesmerized by its amorous delicacy

But, a few days later,
in a traumatic evening,
the flower had withered
Its splendour vanished
in a yellowish brown pallor
Petals not vigorous enough
to bear the dews and about to fall apart
And the sepals dried off
No bees to dash above the dead stigma
Thus the once glorious flower had faded away.

from a Sri Lankan garden

Joan McNerney
Wintry Bouquet

This December
during wide nights
hemmed by blackness,
I remember roses.
Pink yellow red violet
those satin blooms of June.

We must wait six months
before seeing blossoms,
touch their brightness
crush their scent
with fingertips.

Now there are only
ebony pools of winter's
heavy ink of darkness.

Dipping into memory of
my lips touching petals
tantalizing sweet buds.
My body longs for softness.

I glimpse brilliant faces of
flowers right before me as I
burrow beneath frosty blankets.
Bracing against that long, cold
nocturnal of wind and shadow.

from an American garden

Ian Mole
Prunus Blossom Bottle

Black flower sprays
beneath a green glaze.
This sounds like a cocktail
from lost summer days.
Exotically lingering
through history's haze
to feed my eyes
and just amaze.

from an English garden

Duncan Morrish
Flowers for My Love

No man had bought her flowers before,
Never turned up with a bouquet, knocking at her door.
She'd been showered with gifts for years,
all the rings of precious metal –
but never something heartfelt, never something truly special.
I saw the longing inside her, that others did not see –
perhaps I'm glad the first she had, was a little bunch from me.
I had no occasion to buy them for, but to ease her loving heart;
knew this gift would make her feel we could never be apart.
She told me they were gorgeous as she released a happy sigh,
but they were nowhere near as gorgeous
as the sparkles in her eyes.
I'll never forget the moment that she took my gift with joy,
Her faith in love and romance, restored by her loving boy.

from an English garden

Ceri Naz
Chuppah

you are
a flower
in full bloom
petals sheen
so dearly welcoming
a canopy of euphoria
a trance of stargazers
an open sky
of embroidered chambers
in narcosis
in felicity
i remember
a blooming rose
in a mother's heart

from a Filipino garden

Ashraf V. Nediyanad
God

God made flowers
To create love
In the heart of humans
But angels
Took them away
To decorate their wings

from an Indian garden

Bozena Helena Mazur-Nowak
Sunflowers

you sowed sunflowers in the spring
saying: this is my love for you
up to the sky they will grow

I just believed

they grew proudly looking at the sky
sun caressed them flirtatiously
only you are no longer here

looking through the window I froze so sad

I've been waiting

he'll be back I did pray

day after day passed

I tore all of them out today
and buried them at a crossroads
with spring, new ones will probably grow
but not for me anymore ...

from an English garden

Afzal Nusker
A Dewy Rosebud

Blushing
rouge complexion,
wearing a crimson robe;
bathing in fountain of youth the-
fresh dew.

from an Indian garden

Amy S. Pacini
Nature's Gem

Nothing has graced my presence
With more loveliness than the rose
Her ruby petals saturate the air
With gentle passion
Enticing buzzing bees
To kiss her sweet lips
And hummingbirds to nest
Upon her fragrant leaves
She caresses nature
Like a newborn baby
With blooming love
Nurturing her buds
With tender care
Sheltering the earth
With divine beauty
Spreading everlasting joy
With her affectionate aroma
There is no one like her
She is a floral goddess
A delicate silhouette
Radiating with majestic splendour and refined charm.

from an American garden

Grace Pasco
Orchid

You are the most
temperamental orchid I have ever come across.
By the window? You're too cold.
On the table? There's just not enough sun.
You prefer the spot right in front
of the big screen TV.

You're obviously near-sighted. Look-
I can't stand worrying about you every day.
Will you or won't you stay alive?
I arrive and one bud wilts while the other flourishes.

It confuses me so much!
One touch of heat makes you wither
The slightest breeze? You shrivel up?
What... the fuck?!

You are the most
Difficult floral décor
I have ever had the pleasure of watering.
Once a week, I make sure there's no standing water.
So why? Won't you open up to me?

I reread the instructions attached to your vase,
In case, just in case, I just happen to have missed a tip from the fine print.
I wish you to be in mint condition, baby,
Give me hints on how to best help because

Signs of rot or decay sadden me.
Does your chlorophyll let you get your fill of sunlight?
I hear it's the blue portion of the electromagnetic spectrum
That soaks up the most brightness,

But you're just so

The Poetry of Flowers

Self-absorbed sometimes,
And damn right, I did some research.
On how to urge you to be less capricious.
You're making me a pernickety person.

I'm finicky and fussy taking particularly nit-picky measures with you.
Your roots look parched and 'bout ready to break,
No, don't fake it with me.
I can't take that kind of tomfoolery.

Do or do not, there is no trial and error basis for this.
Beautiful, as you are, it's my patience you're pushing.
And yes, you caught me -
I'm no botanist.
But I can sing a few bars for you,

Maybe say a few prayers for you,
Speak to you with care and
Be on my tiptoes for your growth and progress.
I could herald the patron saint of plants for you,

But you won't catch me holding my breath for you.
I got my own roots to respect
My own bloom to see through.
I, too, need vitamin D in my pores to keep calcium intact.

It's a fact that you are the most
Facetious, flippant, flower
With such pigmentation you'd think was just a figment of imaginary poofage,
But you're the proof that you can stand just fine by yourself

Without attention from yours truly.
You are truly an optical magnet in the room,
A significant topical component that assumes
A sight to behold despite the brevity of your life expectancy.

You make now look vibrant

The Poetry of Flowers

And soon look promising.
You make home feel less lonely
And your saucer worthy of complete and undivided awareness.

Your petals are precious and so are your stems.
You make movement toward being a grown-up
And in full-form look damn right majestic.
You're not just planted on the ground, you've stuck a perfect landing.

Me? I'm just grateful that you have such patience.
With my impatience and insistence.
From this poem on, I'll meet you at your pace.

Roses are red.
Orchids can be shades and hues of violet and blue.
You make my life better,
Even though you prefer the spot right in front of the big screen TV,

Obviously, you're worth it.

from an American garden

Akshaya Pawaskar
Flower Picker

Shadow sits in the
Bower of a tree
Rhizomes hold it up
What goes on below?
The veins and arteries,
The plasma of the leaves.

Collect some sprigs
These mini trees'
Offspring, several
Like tadpoles they bunch
Like caterpillars winged,
They fly over gardens.

Gardens, gardens
Nosegay and corsages
They dance, light
Fastened on dainty
Wrists of partners.
They sit smug.

On table tops in
Vases deep, but
not the same earth
Not feeling at home.
Distant giggles,
Drunken tumbles.
Party slackens

Left is a carnage;
Carnage of flowers
of love, of beauty
The sillage, incense
Soon a nonentity.

from an Indian garden

Elisavietta Ritchie
Floricultural Traditions: Warning

Two tiny daffodils beyond the compost bin!
No one will miss them...First of this spring...
I reach through the briars—Yet two?

Russian tradition: an even count
signifies someone has died, odd numbers
of blooms in a vase for the living.

I won't invite Death, here too often as is,
will add these two to the big daffodil
in the glass on my windowsill...Ergo three.

Yet all around: cherry trees, apple, pear,
plum trees flower, their blossom counts
even and odd...Who's counting?

So we celebrate the living, honour the dead
who live on in these blooming trees,
funeral wreaths or bridal bouquets in the sky.

from an American garden

Elisavietta Ritchie
Lilacs

Lilacs have bloomed here 200 years
though the house burned a decade ago.

Hedges divided the vegetable garden
and yard where laundry was hung

from the boisterous peony beds
people still come to admire.

I should cut the deadwood. Instead,
I bury my nose in lavender spires.

Generations of grandmothers burst
from the heart-shaped leaves.

Each has her tale of how he courted her
under these lilacs, their miniature

stamens glistening and pistils leering,
or how she played here as a child

while her grandma hung out the wash,
took in an apron full of asparagus spears,

and how, just beyond the hedge, a wolf lurked,
or a man exposed himself to her curious eyes,

so for all her life, and mine,
the fragrance of lilacs was not

handkerchiefs trimmed with lace
but shirt tails damp in the April wind.

from an American garden

Elspeth C. Ritchie
Pumpkin Flowers

Yellow blossoms glow
between large fans of
leaves. Vines spill
past nasturtium bounds
into the shaggy lawn.

I should mow, weed,
neaten my unkempt Eden.
But pumpkin tendrils
grab the passive grass,
strangling out sun.

Morning glories ride
my fences, violet
blossoms radiating dawn,
spreading sunrise up
into the tree above.

Their heart-shaped leaves
tangle the baby tomatoes;
I snip their life lines.

How do you choose between
the flower and the fruit?

A young tulip poplar
shoots up strait
shading golden mums.
Too close to my home,
his roots threaten bricks.
Finally, I chainsaw him down.

In therapy I also dig,
scoop at resistance or
rake memories towards the dawn.

The Poetry of Flowers

I edge the boundaries on
the psychiatric ward,
locking doors,
granting passes,
keeping blades away
from soft untended arms.

In a herb garden,
stray tomatoes become
weeds to be pulled,
so dill can wave green
feathers at the sky.

May my hands fertilize
medicinal leaves,
sweet berries and
glory-giving blooms.

from an American garden

Bethany Rivers
Heart-flower

daffodil emanating sunshine
from dawn till dusk – a subtle musk
plays between shades of wine
usually the second sign of life returning

tiny trumpets exude news of life
narcissi who listen to the heart's faint voice
two-tone spellbinders with dragon tongues
converge on verges resolute
in growing the aisle of spring

ready to wed you
to the world again

from an English garden

Vincent Van Ross
Led by the Nose

It was an adventure trip
That took a fragrant turn
A mild scent wafting from the flower
Led me by my nose

It was a bush with a medium-sized
Green leaves from which
Little white buds were trying to
Burst into blooms

The scent was intoxicating
It was heady mix of fragrance
That forced me to kneel down
And sniff at source of this scent

I found it in the wild
But, it can grow in the garden
The fragrance of jasmine
Can bind everyone into a spell

from an Indian garden

Ceò Ruaírc

Vernal Observance

Fiddlehead ferns play
Sweet music of Spring
our albedo bodies
running like Jesus Lizards
above Stokum Falls
Vancouver Island sun
beats down
on slowly ripening buds
Cedars sing to this return
Pink fawn lilies
bow in the breeze
to unnamed deities
we swirl and twirl
like whirligig beetles
or resilient seeds spinning
on the wind
as if dancing
were the only sane response
to this raw beauty
this green joy
Cottonwood's sweet balsamic scent
surrounds us
Trillium
opens its white petals to the sky

from a Canadian garden

Miriam Sagan
Fortuna's Garden

I take your hand along the mossy way
Camellia blossoms fall, the red Japonica
That brings to mind a viewing with a parasol;
Inside a winding glade a statue stands—
A saint, a goddess, or a grave.

Once I was young, and dreamed
I held a globe of water in my hands—
It shattered, and a cardinal, red bird,
Flew out and lighted in the grove's pale trees.

Red petals punctuate my thoughts
And make me want to kiss
Your lips again, worn soft
By time, and mine.

Within the boxwood maze
An unseen peacock's cry
Whose Argos eyes fan out yet still can't see.
White camellia, scentless,
Settles down like snow
And jonquils springing from cool ground
Evoke what might have been—
What I know now
That once I did not know.

from an American garden

Neethu Sasikumar
Morning Delight

What joy did my garden bring?
To the misty morning of this spring.
With immensely beautiful and agile
Myriad of flowers lined with a smile.

Sunflowers always stood upright
A wish so warm: Oh! What a delight?
Blossoms dropped; pink, yellow and red
Blooming down from a fine woven thread.

Dahlias dazzled beaded with dew
Roses sprayed perfume sweet and new
A naughty sunflower popped out her tongue
To mock my posture; dreamy and dumb.

More life did that sunshine bring
To my garden in this spring.
A symphony from an old rusty string
Blush on a bee who forgot to sing.

from an Indian garden

Don Schaeffer
Introduction to Photographs of Flowers

As an entertainer
I don't often
write about flowers.
I don't own them.
They are never
original and thus
are never true.
They don't push
against the friction
of my mind properly.
However, they are the
sex organs of
our neighbours, the
vegetables. They
model the most
important part
of our swift passage
over the years with their
fresh beginnings and their
fading.
They mean
what we do
quietly. But
they state it
grandly, with
pretty smells.
We hide in them,
even use them to
draw each other
into our dark and
private corners.

from an American garden

Sunil Sharma
Adornment

On slender stripped branches
Blossom the white flowers,
Soon to die;
The champa in big clusters,
Blooming on the bald tree;
Nature has covered amply
The tree's shocking bareness;
The white adding tender colour to
The stark brown of the stunted tree;
A marvellous sight in the wilderness,
For the urban eyes, looking for relief!

from an Indian garden

Eleanor Sivins
Where They Belonged

The store bought flowers watched over the street,
Gazing at every movement,
Longing for their non-existent feet,
Reaching up to the only sun they could gather.

The buds began to bloom,
As they drank each drop of water,
Only to realize they were in one room,
Nowhere near their nature.

Each flower began to wither,
Within days of their arrival,
And as they moved beyond the window,
There was a gasp of survival.

Placed among the grasses and seeds,
They seemed to decay for the better,
Their bodies becoming one again,
Never to falter or fetter.

from an English garden

Dennis Trujillo
Sunrise Altar

Like Noah's impulse to build an ark
I woke with a glint in my heart

And drove to Home Depot to buy
A wooden trellis and two

Packets of morning glory seeds—
Small and black like the eyes of bees.

The sun and I partnered for weeks—
Performed our duties tenderly.

Me with silver mists of water—
The sun with golden bundles of light.

Clinging vines with heart-shaped leaves
Soon twined the trellis green.

And when funnel-shaped blooms burst
Into colour—purple, pink, and blue—

The trellis sparkled like a sunrise altar
That could be seen from the farthest star.

from an American garden

Bhisma Upreti
Flower Garden and Mind

Whichever flower garden I am in
Flowers do not name themselves
Neither do they bother who I am.

Whenever I am there
they smile as if with kith and kin
And make me smile
As rain washes the dust away
from tree leaves.
So their smile relieves my agony and despair.

When I wish for a fresh, pure and brilliant mind
I go towards the flower garden.

from a Nepalese garden

Sylvia Riojas Vaughn
Manet: Peonies in a Vase

His favourite flowers.
Born of common earth,
top heavy
yet rendered on canvas
as delicate, ethereal,
almost floating
above glossy ceramic.
One splendid fallen bloom
nudges eternity.
Translucent colours
reminiscent of the sea —
fragile mother of pearl,
pink blush of conch shells,
leaves green as mermaids' tears.
Hardy perennials
resistant to transplant,
homebodies like the artist
who couldn't leave his muse in Paris.
Like the Parisians he painted,
like his garden's beauties,
he blossomed
where sown.

from an American garden

Sylvia Riojas Vaughn
Stars in My Garden

Weeding nose to petal
amid a bounty of Oriental lilies,
the spicy scent evokes
perfumed memories
of moonlit kisses.
Brilliant pink and creamy white
blossoms, glossy foliage,
so right for a corsage.
Stunning.
I forget my sore back.
I close my eyes,
picture the night
far from street lamps.
Overhead, twinkling lights
that children draw
in shapes like these flowers.
How marvellous, this
constellation on Earth

from an American garden

Lita Verella
Scent of a Rose

Divine breath of ambrosia
From a distance beckoning me
Towards flushed blooms
Afoot in the glen
Their sweetness
Carried along in the wind
Savoured by the senses
This alluring treat
My eyes now close
A sigh is slowly released

from an American garden

Marion de Vos
Pheromones

Shamelessly they quiver
in Spring breeze
like pink tongues
of panting dogs.
lust for sun,
breathe out those
invisible vapours
to seduce
their pollinating lovers.
no conscience,
those flowers,
or is there?

Animals phlegm,
a grimace
on their faces,
curl their upper lip
like a smile,
bare their teeth,
not for aggression,
but for the scent of love.

It seems,
we humans
send those signals
without knowing.

from an American garden

John Ward
Ikebana

It's not really a man thing though is it?
A bit like crying not very manly
My routine for this is pretty well set
(One that I'd rather not have to be in)
Saturday always seemed like a good day
A little bit more restful after Friday
Peaceful but not so quiet as Sunday
Not a choice I ever wanted to make
On the whole I'd much rather be shopping
Which is saying something if you know me
It's not just putting flowers in a pot
It's about working with the living things
About sustaining a closeness, about love
That's flower arranging on Saturdays

from an English garden

Robert West
Survivor

O daisy
dazed and

dizzy in
what seems

like endless
wind, who

wouldn't praise
you? you

who hold
your ground,

and somehow
too your

lovely head
so high.

from an American garden

Heidi Willson
Withered Rose

Depleting beauty,
existing only for ridicule,
fading petals hanging on,
bowing in submission,
dew dripping down,
crying lonely tears,
flawed among perfect beauty,
withering slowly
suffering its last moments
of life

from an American garden

Abigail Wyatt
Lady Convolvulus

Pretty as a picture in white and pink,
Lady Convolvulus lifts up her head;
the jewels of the morning adorn her cheeks
and her green gown winds about her legs.

And My Lady creeps and My Lady runs;
on a summer wind she blows.
She tilts her chin to kiss the sun
and follows where he goes.

And My Lady sighs and My Lady weeps;
and My Lady cleaves and clings;
and she binds up her lover and, where he sleeps,
a green and fecund web she spins

from an English garden

Abigail Wyatt
Valerian

Once pretty in pink
you are innocent no longer
but frowsy now under the sun.
Your head lolls
like a drowsing drunk's
towards the lulling,
dull oblivion of sleep.
Briefly you flourished
where the old wall cracks,
your slender roots
fingering this dust.
Now you dig down deep
for the cooling dark,
grimly holding out,
holding on.

from an English garden

The Poetry of Flowers

Acknowledgements

DR NICOLE ANTOINE: 'Yoni' from *AllPoetry.com* (2016) reprinted by permission of the poet. DEBBI BRODY: 'Collinsia Verna', from *Not Drowning (Waving*), (2007), reprinted by permission of the poet. GIBSON, CLEVELAND W.: 'Surreal Mind Garden', from *Cool and Quirky,* (2008), reprinted by permission of the poet. ALICJA KUBERSKA: 'Spring in the Garden' and 'Sunflower' from *(Not) My Poem,* (2015), reprinted by permission of the poet. INDUNIL MADHUSANKHA: 'The Fate of a Beautiful Flower' from *Moonlight Dreamers of Yellow Haze*, (2016), reprinted by permission of the poet. BOZENA HELENA MAZUR-NOWAK: 'Sunflowers' from *Blue Longing* (2014), reprinted by permission of the poet. GRACE PASCO: 'Orchid', from *The Foliate Oak Literary Magazine,* (http://www.foliateoak.com, 2016*),* reprinted by permission of the poet. ELISAVIETTA RITCHIE: 'Lilacs' from *The Arc of the Storm,* (Signal Books, Feb. 1998), reprinted by permission of the poet. ELSPETH C. RITCHIE: 'Pumpkin Flowers' from *Journal of the American Medication Association,* (25 August 1993), reprinted by permission of poet. P. J. REED: 'the august sorrows', 'cool breezes whisper', 'whispers of summer,' and 'poor yellow flower', from *Haiku Nation*, (Lost Tower Publications, 2015), 'green fresh wrapped petals' from Haiku Yellow, (Lost Tower Publications, 2016), reprinted by permission of the poet. ROBERT WEST: 'Survivor' from *Alabama Literary Review*, (Vol. 19, no.1, 2010), reprinted by permission of the poet. ABIGAIL WYATT: 'Lady Convolvulus' from *Hysteria 1* (ed. Linda Parkinson-Hardman, 2013), reprinted by permission of the poet.

Artwork

Page	Artist
Cover Art	The Front and Back pages of this anthology were designed by **Jasmine Reed-Yang**, an undergraduate student from Exeter University.
	'Follow Your Own Path' by **Elena Ray**. The picture is of a snail climbing a flower and is a mixed medium collage. Elena Ray comes from Joshua Tree, USA. She creates photography, mixed medium art, and photo illustration.
12	*Black Rose* by **Veronika Surovtseva**. A watercolour painting of a rose painted in an Asian style.
16	*Lotus Flowers* by **Veronika Surovtseva**. An original watercolour painting of a lotus.
88	*Lotus Blossom* by **Vincent Go**. A vector illustration of a lotus blossom painting.

Bibliography

Evolutionary Psychology, Eds. Shackelford, T., Fink, B., Puts, D., Sear, R., 2016 Release of Journal Citation Reports, Source: 2015 Web of Science Data, Sage Publications.

Farr, J., (2004), *The Gardens of Emily Dickinson,* Harvard: Harvard College.

Lambert, T. (2014), *A Brief History of Gardening.* Available from http://www.localhistories.org/gardening.html [Accessed on 05/09/2016]

Nadel, D. (2005) in Balter, M. (2013) Saying It With Flowers, 14,000 Years Ago, *Science Magazine.* Available from: http://www.sciencemag.org/news/2013/07/saying-it-flowers-14000-years-ago [Accessed on 05/09/2016]

Royal Horticultural Society, 2015, School Gardening; *Flowers in Shakespeare's Plays,* Available from https://schoolgardening.rhs.org.uk/Resources/Info-Sheet/Flowers-in-Shakespeare-s-Plays [Accessed on 05/09/2016]

Rufus, Q.C. (c.100 AD), Full Text from Archives of 'Seven Wonders of the Ancient World,' *History of Alexander,* Volume.1.35-5. Available at https://archive.org/stream/SevenWondersOfTheAncientWorld/SevenWondersOfTheAncientWorld_djvu.txt [Accessed on 05/09/2016]

Wordsworth, W., c. 1800, found at BrainyQuote.com, Xplore Inc, 2016.
http://www.brainyquote.com/quotes/quotes/w/williamwor147034.html, [Accessed on 10/09/2016]

Biography of Poets

Sheikha A. is from Pakistan and the United Arab Emirates. Over 300 of her poems appear in a variety of print and online venues including several anthologies by different presses. More about her can be accessed at sheikha82.wordpress.com She edits poetry for *eFiction, India*.

Kimmy Alan is a wannabe poet from the land of Lake Woebegone. A retired steel worker who was diagnosed with stage 4 cancer, Kimmy Alan pursed his love of poetry as a distraction while undergoing chemo and radiation. For him, poetry has proven to be a powerful catharsis as he is currently in remission. When he isn't writing he spends time with his four wonderful nieces, whom he says 'are driving him to pieces.'

Jasmine Allen lives in scenic north Idaho. Out of the many things in life that she enjoys, poetry and opera are her primary passions. She also loves art and politics. Allen feels that she is best able to express her deepest beliefs and emotions through her passions. In the poem, 'Undying Love', Allen expresses the emotions attached to true love. Forget-me-nots are used to symbolize this concept in the poem. The idea for the poem came to the poet in a dream one night. In the dream, she was in a burning house caused by a falling star. Allen states that she did not feel afraid, however, because she was brought comfort by the glowing forget-me-nots that fell from the sky. The nostalgia felt from the flowers made her feel that all was alright, even in the face of destruction.

Dr Nicole Lewis Antoine is a professor of education and English at Houston Community College-SW. She has over 10 years in education and continues to grow in her field. Dr Antoine enjoys all forms of writing, but her passion for poetry keeps her motivated and fulfilled in her life. Writing poetry is her therapy.

Born in Oshkosh, WI, a resident of Ossining, NY, poet **Donna Barkman** was born into a family of actors and has continued that tradition, while adding the writing of poetry and short

The Poetry of Flowers

plays to her repertoire. Her poetry has been published in *Chautauqua*, *The Westchester Review*, *Common Ground*, *Pennsylvania English* and *Adrienne Rich, A Tribute Anthology* along with many others, and has been performed by her at the Hudson Valley Center for Contemporary Art in Peekskill, NY and in galleries in Westchester and New York City.

A Pushcart nominee, **Lana Bella** is an author of two chapbooks, *Under My Dark* (Crisis Chronicles Press, 2016) and *Adagio* (Finishing Line Press, forthcoming), and has had poetry and fiction featured with over 280 journals including *2River*, *California Quarterly*, *Chiron Review*, *Columbia Journal*, *Poetry Salzburg Review*, *San Pedro River Review*, *The Hamilton Stone Review*, *The Ilanot Review*, *The Writing Disorder, Third Wednesday, Tipton Poetry Journal, Yes Poetry,* and *Elsewhere,* among others. She resides in the US and the coastal town of Nha Trang, Vietnam, where she is a mom of two far-too-clever-frolicsome imps.

For more information, visit her Facebook page at https://www.facebook.com/Lana-Bella-789916711141831

Mary Bone has had poems published in magazines, journals, newspapers and online blogs.

Debbi Brody is an avid attendee and leader of workshops throughout the Southwest, USA. She has been published in numerous national and regional journals, magazines, and anthologies of note including *Poetica, Broomweed*, and *Sin Fronteras.* Her newest full length poetry book, *In Everything, Birds,* (Village Books Press, OKC, OK, 2015) is available at Independent bookstores across the US and at the usual online purchase sites.

Lissie Bull is from Bristol, England and has been published in a few other anthologies. She loves to paint pictures through the use of words from the heart. She has a blog with other 1200 poems: lissiebullpoetry.blogspot.co.uk.

Wanda Morrow Clevenger is a Carlinville, IL native. Over 386 pieces of her work appear or are forthcoming in 137 print and electronic journals and anthologies. She has a book entitled *This Same Small Town in Each of Us*.

Mariela Cordero is a Lawyer, Poet, Writer and Visual Artist. Her poetry awards include, Third Poetry Prize *Pizarnik*

Argentina (2014), First Prize in the *II Iberoamerican Poetry Contest*, Euler Granda, Ecuador (2015), Second Prize for Poetry in *Concorso Letterario Internazionale Bilingual Tracceperlameta Edizioni,* Italy (2015), and First Prize for Micropoems in *Castilian Transpalabrarte*, Spain (2015).

Philip Dodd lives in Liverpool, England, and is the author of three books, *Angel War, Klubbe the Turkle and the Golden Star Coracle,* and *Still the Dawn: Poems and Ballads*. His poem, 'The Redundancy of Gods', was published in *Greek Fire*, by Lost Tower Publications.

Fathima E.V. is a writer and translator from Kerala, India, with modest publishing credits for poems and fiction in anthologies and international journals. She was the winner of the *Vocabula Well Written Prose Contest*, 2011, for creative prose. Her translation *A Preface to Man* was published by Harper Collins in May 2016.

Kaitlyn Fox is a 16-year-old poet living in Grand Rapids, Michigan. She has held a passion for writing starting at a young age, continuing to channel her thoughts through her poetry and lyrics.

Mark Frank has a number of poems published in different anthologies in Britain, America and South Africa. His latest poems referred as the Haseenic Poems are his latest reflection of love.

Eric Harvey is a 64-year-old who has written poetry for the past 5 years. He has a portfolio of about three hundred poems with five published, but is currently working on an anthology of WW1 poems.

Cleveland W. Gibson is a writer and poet. He has an audio book out and photo art online. His work in progress is a book of 75 poems and a novel called the *House of the Skull Drum*.

Norbert Gora is a 26-year old poet and writer from the little town of Góra, Poland. Many of his horror, Sci-Fi and romance short stories have been published in his home country. He is also the author of many poems in English-language poetry anthologies around the world.

Kristyl Gravina is from the island of Malta. Her work has appeared in several publications including *The Black Rose of Winter*, *Greek Fire* and *Temptation* by Lost Tower Publications as well as *The Literary Hatchet*, *Haiku Journal* and *Hindered Souls* among others.

Carol Lynn Grellas is an eight-time Pushcart nominee as well as a four-time Best of the Net nominee. She is the 2012 winner of the Red Ochre Press Chapbook contest with her manuscript *Before I Go to Sleep*. She has authored several chapbooks along with her latest full-length collection of poems: *Hasty Notes in No Particular Order*, released from Aldrich Press in 2013. Her work has appeared in a wide variety of online and print magazines including: *The Yale Journal for Humanities in Medicine*, *Poets and Artists*, *War, Literature and the Arts,* and many more. According to family lore she is a direct descendent of Robert Louis Stevenson, **www.clgrellaspoetry.com**

Debbie Johnson is an author/poet from the US. She is disabled and writes for both therapy and enjoyment. She has published three books on disability; *The Disability Experience, The Disability Experience II, and Debbie's Friends*, a book for children. These are collections of both non-fiction and poetry. More information can be found at
www.thedisabilityexperience.vpweb.com

Wendy Joseph has sailed cargo ships as a deckhand worldwide, and lives in the wilds of Washington State.

Tim Kahl [http://www.timkahl.com] is the author of *Possessing Yourself* (CW Books, 2009), *The Century of Travel* (CW Books, 2012) and *The String of Islands* (Dink, 2015). His work has been published in *Prairie Schooner, Drunken Boat, Mad Hatters' Review, Indiana Review, Metazen, Ninth Letter, Sein und Werden, Notre Dame Review, The Really System, Konundrum Engine Literary Magazine, The Journal, The Volta, Parthenon West Review, Caliban* and many other journals in the U.S. He appears as Victor Schnickelfritz at the poetry and poetics blog *The Great American Pinup* (http://greatamericanpinup.wordpress.com/) and the poetry video blog *Linebreak Studios* [http://linebreakstudios.blogspot.com/]. He is also editor of *Bald Trickster Press* and *Clade Song* [http://www.cladesong.com]. He is the vice president and events coordinator of The Sacramento Poetry Center. He also has a public installation in Sacramento {In Scarcity We Bare The Teeth} [http://www.flickr.com/photos/rickele/11129585563/] [http://www.sacmetroarts.org/documents/FullPoems.pdf] He currently teaches at California State University, Sacramento.

Kaikasi V.S. is presently working as Asst. Professor of English, University College, Thiruvananthapuram. She has been actively involved in teaching English Language and Literature for the past six years. She is the recipient of the prestigious 'Best Young Educationalist' Award instituted by the Rotary Club International in the year 2015. She has also to her credit several articles both in English and Malayalam published in peer reviewed journals and other publications. She has more than 30 paper presentations both National and International and has also been invited for several lectures and training programmes. Her area of research is Indian Mythology and is equally interested in translating literary works in her mother tongue. Her passions include reading and writing poems, stories and critical pieces both in literature and films. As a student she has received the 'Sargaprathibha' Endowment prize for Government College of Teacher Education, Thiruvananthapuram for excellence in literature. She is at present engaged in writing a re-telling of the Ramayana from Ravana's mother's perspective. She is also a selected member of the New Initiatives Programme of Govt. of Kerala including Walk With the Scholar, Scholar Support Programme, Additional Skill Acquisition Programme and FLAIR. She is also an accomplished poet whose poems have been published in several international and national journals.

Linda Kraus has taught literature and film studies at the university level. She has published poetry in several literary journals and anthologies and is currently editing two collections of poems. She is an orchid judge, a rock hound and a film buff.

Richard Krawiec teaches online courses for UNC Chapel Hill, for which he won their Excellence in Teaching Award in 2009. He is founder of Jacar Press, a Community Active publishing company www.jacarpress.com that publishes full-length collections, chapbooks, anthologies and an award-winning online magazine at http://one.jacarpress.com. He has worked extensively with people in homeless shelters, women's shelters, prisons, literacy classes, and community sites, teaching writing.

Alicja Maria Kuberska is a poetess, novelist, journalist, editor and member of the Polish Writers Associations in Warsaw, Poland. She was born in 1960, in Świebodzin, Poland, now residing in Inowrocław, Poland.

In 2011 she published her 1st volume of poems entitled, *The Glass Reality.* Her 2nd volume *Analysis of Feelings*, was published in 2012. The 3rd collection *Moments* was published in English in 2014, both in Poland and in the USA. In 2014, she also published the novel - *Virtual Roses* and volume of poems *On the Border of Dream*. In 2015 her volume entitled *Girl in the Mirror* was published in the UK and she edited another anthology entitled *The Other Side of the Screen*; in 2016 she edited another anthology *Love is Like Air* and two volumes of poetry: love poems entitled *Taste of Love* (in English) and *Thief of Dreams* (in Polish).
Her poems have been published in numerous anthologies and magazines in Poland, Belgium, USA, UK, Canada, India, Israel, Italy and Australia.

John Lambremont Sr is a poet from Baton Rouge, Louisiana,

USA. John's poems have been published in such journals as *Pacific Review, Clarion*, and the *Minetta Review* and he has been nominated for the Pushcart Prize. John's new book *The Moment of Capture* is forthcoming from Lit Fest Press in June 2017.

Joan Leotta is an internationally published journalist, Author, performer, and poet. She lives and writes by the beach in Calabash, NC

Indunil Madhusankha is a budding young poet from Sri Lanka. He is currently an undergraduate reading for a BSc Special Degree in Mathematics in the Faculty of Science of the University of Colombo and he takes a great interest in the subjects of Mathematics, Statistics, and Computer Science. Indunil compiled his first collection of poetry entitled, *Oasis*, when he was sixteen and he is currently working on his second collection, *Reflections of Life* and also on a book titled, *A Rare Kind of beauty, Yet Unexplored: A Selection of Modern Sri Lankan Sinhala Poetry* featuring a translation of a set of select Sinhala poems written by some famous Sri Lankan poets. Moreover, his creative and academic works have been featured in many international journals, magazines, websites and anthologies in the United States, United Kingdom, Canada, Africa, Nigeria, India, Sri Lanka and some other countries

Joan McNerney's poetry has been included in numerous literary magazines such as *Seven Circle Press, Dinner with the Muse, Moonlight Dreamers of Yellow Haze, Blueline,* and *Halcyon Days.* Three Bright Hills Press Anthologies, several Poppy Road Review Journals, and numerous Kind of A Hurricane Press Publications have accepted her work. Her latest title is *Having Lunch with the Sky* and she has four Best of the Net nominations.

The Poetry of Flowers

Ian Mole was born in Sunderland but has lived in London for many years. He is a teacher of English to overseas students and a tour guide.

Duncan Morrish is an English Language under graduate from Cardiff University.

Caroline Nazareno-Gabis a.k.a. **Ceri Naz,** was born in Anda, Pangasinan and is known as a 'poet of peace and friendship.' She is a multi-award winning poet, editor, publicist, linguist, educator, and women's advocate.

She graduated *cum laude* with a Bachelor of Elementary Education degree from Pangasinan State University, specializing in General Science. She been a voracious researcher in various arts, science and literature, volunteering at the Richmond Multicultural Concerns Society, TELUS World Science, Vancouver Art Gallery, and Vancouver Aquarium.

She is privileged to have be chosen as one of the Directors of Writers Capital International Foundation (WCIF), one of the Board of Directors of Galaktika ATUNIS Magazine based in Albania; the World Poetry Canada and International Director to Philippines; Global Citizen's Initiatives Member, Asia Pacific Writers and Translators (APWT 2015 member); Association for Women's rights in Development (AWID) and Anacbanua. She has been published in various international anthologies.

She has received prestigious awards including, 4th Place in the *World Union of Poets Poetry Prize*, Writers International Network- Canada, 'Amazing Poet 2015', The *Frang Bardhi Literary Prize 2014* (Albania), the *sair-gazeteci or Poet-Journalist Award 2014* (Tuzla, Istanbul, Turkey) and *World Poetry Empowered Poet 2013* (Vancouver, Canada).

Ashraf V. Nediyanad works as a Senior Clerk in the Calicut Municipal Corporation Office in Kerala, India.
He writes his poems in English, whilst his stories are in

Malayalam. Various magazines and anthologies have published his work, including Lost Tower Publications and Ardus British Columbia. He is married with two children and lives in Narikkuni.

Bozena Helena Mazur-Nowak was born in Poland. In search of work she migrated to the UK. Her poems were published on web portals and in numerous anthologies worldwide. Much of the work of this poet can be found on her Facebook profile. The poet has released six volumes of poetry. Her awards include the *Poets Gratitude Award 2014*, *Organic Work Award 2015* for her contribution to Polish Culture and the *Stanislav Moniuszko statuette* for her dedication to her Polish roots and dissemination of her culture worldwide. Her poetry publications are *on the bank of river called life* (2011) *ticket to the happiness station* (2012*), on the departure bridge* (2013), *Whispered* (2013), *Blue Longing* (2014), *Cormorants Will Return* (2015) and *DOOM: a Short Story Collection.*

Afzal Nusker was born in (1985) and brought up in Kolkata, India. After High School, He opted for Interior Designing from Ex-In, Designing Institute. He works as a professional interior designer, but has always had an inclination towards Literature. Nusker's passion for literary content encouraged him to write poems. He is a member of **PoetrySoup.com** where more of his writing can be found.

Amy S. Pacini is a freelance writer and poet based in Land O Lakes, Florida. Her work has been widely published in online ezines, literary journals and anthologies. She is a two-time 1st place winner of the *Annual Romancing The Craft of Poetry & Fiction Contest* for 2013-14 sponsored by the TL Publishing Group, and is 2015 Pushcart Prize nominee. Pacini writes poetry, short stories, personal essays and motivational quotes. Visit her website at www.amyspacini.com.

Grace Pasco is a spoken word poet from Silver Spring, Maryland. Find her on Instagram as GoshGracious.

The Poetry of Flowers

Priya Patel is a writer, poet, and lover of words. She has a story to tell and wants the world to hear it. Her biography is written between the soft syllables and sounds that you hear when you read her work.

Akshaya Pawaskar is a doctor from Goa, India who dabbles in poetry in her spare time. She has been published in *Writer's ezine*, *eFiction India* and by Lost Tower Publications.

P.J. Reed is a writer and poet from England. She is an eclectic writer. Her work has appeared in a wide variety of online and print magazines including *Five to One* magazine, *Ealain* magazine, *Indiana Voice Journal*, *Whirlwind, cattails,* and the *Haiku Journal*. In 2015 she was short listed for the National Poetry Anthology award.

She has published one collection of dark romantic and Gothic horror poetry entitled *The Wicked Come*. Her high fantasy novel *The Torcian Chronicles* will be published in 2017.

As a counterbalance to her dark writing, P.J. also writes of the beauty and ethereal nature of the changing countryside in her series of haiku inspired collections *Haiku Nation* (2015), *Frozen Haiku* (2016) and *Haiku Yellow* (2016).

Explore her writing at http://wickedpoetry.jigsy.com

P.J. Reed is on Twitter at: https://twitter.com/PJReed_author

Elisavietta Ritchie's fiction, poetry, creative non-fiction, photojournalism, and translations from Russian, French, Malay and Indonesian have appeared in numerous publications. Her books include, *Babushka's Beads: A Geography of Gene, Guy Wires, In Haste I Write You This Note, Stories & Half-Stories* (print & e-book), New collection *Glad I Gave to Art My All* (poems on paintings, in the voices of the artist, his wife, mistress, dog;) in production.

Dr. Elspeth Ritchie is a forensic psychiatrist with especial expertise in military and veteran's issues. She recently joined the Washington DC VA, as Chief of the Community Based

Outpatient Clinics. Prior to that assignment, she was the Chief Clinical Officer, Department of Behavioral Health, for the District of Columbia. She retired from the Army in 2010, after holding numerous leadership positions within Army Medicine, to include the Psychiatry Consultant. She trained at Harvard, George Washington, Walter Reed, and the Uniformed Services University of the Health Sciences, and has completed fellowships in both forensic and preventive and disaster psychiatry. She is a Professor of Psychiatry at the Uniformed Services University of the Health Sciences, Georgetown University, George Washington University and Howard University School of Medicine. An internationally recognized expert, she brings a unique public health approach to the management of disaster and combat mental health issues. Her assignments and other missions have taken her to Korea, Somalia, Iraq, and Cuba.

She has over 200 publications, mainly in the areas of forensic, disaster, suicide, ethics, military combat psychiatry, and women's health issues. She is the senior editor on the recently published volumes: *Forensic and Ethical Issues in Military Behavioral Health, Women at War, and Post-Traumatic Stress Disorder and Related Diseases in Combat Veterans: A Clinical Casebook.* Forthcoming books include *Intimacy After Injury: Combat Trauma and Sexual Health* and *Psychiatrists in Combat, Clinicians Experience in the War Zone.*

Other major publications include the Military Medicine Textbook on *Combat and Operational Behavioral Health*, *The Mental Health Response to the 9/11 Attack on the Pentagon*, *Mental Health Interventions for Mass Violence and Disaster*, *Humanitarian Assistance and Health Diplomacy: Military-Civilian Partnership in the 2004 Tsunami Aftermath*, and the 2013 series on *The Use of Complementary and Alternative Medicines for the Treatment of PTSD in Military Service Members.*

Bethany Rivers' debut pamphlet, *Off the wall,* came out in July from Indigo Dreams Publishing. She teaches Creative

Writing and mentors writers through their novels and memoirs. She regularly runs poetry inspiration and healing days. www.writingyourvoice.org.uk

Vincent Van Ross is a journalist and editor based at New Delhi in India. He writes on national and international politics, defense, environment, travel, spirituality and scores of other topics. Apart from this, He dabbles in a little bit of poetry, fiction, non-fiction and humorous writings.

Vincent's articles and features have appeared in over a dozen newspapers and magazines in India and Bangladesh. He is also a renowned photographer and an art critic. His poems are littered in anthologies and journals across the world and on numerous poetry sites and Facebook groups on the web.

Ceò Ruairc is a naturalist and poet, who writes from a small island cabin, inspired by marine life, coastal storms, and the tenacity of trees.

Mariam Sagan is the author of 30 published books, including *Black Rainbow* (Sherman, Asher, 2015) and *Geographic: A Memoir of Time and Space* (Casa de Snapdragon, 2016). She founded and heads the creative writing program at Santa Fe Community College. Her blog *Miriam's Well* (http://miriamswell.wordpress.com) has a thousand daily readers. She has been a writer in residence in two national parks, at Yaddo, MacDowell, Colorado Art Ranch, Andrew's Experimental Forest, Center for Land Use Interpretation, Ice's Gulkistan Residency for creative people, and another dozen or so remote and unique places. Her awards include the *Santa Fe Mayor's award for Excellence in the* Arts, the *Poetry Gratitude Award from New Mexico Literary Arts,* and A *Lannan Foundation residency* in Marfa.

Born and brought up in a small Indian village**, Neethu Sasikumar** loves nature and enjoyed a childhood of dashing through the paddy fields and along the riverside, giving her an admiration of nature along with the lovely life it unveiled throughout my journey into adulthood. She is a M.Tech graduate in Optical Engineering from Indian Institute of Space Science and Technology currently works for a private firm in Bangalore, India.

Don Schaeffer has previously published a dozen volumes of poetry, his first in 1996, not counting the experiments with self-publishing under the name "Enthalpy Press." He spent a lot of his young adult life hawking books and learning the meaning of vanity. His poetry has appeared in numerous periodicals and has been translated into Chinese for distribution abroad. Don is a habitué of the poetry forum network and has received first prize in the Inter-board competition.

Mumbai-based, **Sunil Sharma** writes prose and poetry, apart from doing literary journalism and freelancing. A senior academic, he has been published in some of the leading international journals and anthologies. Sunil has got three collections of poetry, one collection of short fiction, one novel and co-edited five books of poetry, short fiction and literary criticism.

Recipient of the UK-based Destiny Poets, *Inaugural Poet of the Year* award (2012).

Another notable achievement is his select poems were published in the prestigious UN project: *Happiness: The Delight-Tree (2015).*

He edits English section of the monthly *Setu*, a bilingual journal from Pittsburgh, USA:

http://www.setumag.com/p/setu-home.html

Eleanor Sivins is currently an English Undergraduate and aspires to be a writer.

Dennis Trujillo from Pueblo, Colorado, is a former US army soldier and middle/high school mathematics teacher. In 2010, he spontaneously began writing poetry, not knowing where his spark came from. Recent and upcoming publications are with *3Elements Review, Agave, Atlanta Review, The Aurorean, Blast Furnace, KYSO Flash, The Quotable, Spank the Carp, THEMA and Three Drops from a*

Cauldron.

Bhisma Upreti is an award winning Nepali poet and writer. He is the recipient of the First Prize in the *National Poetry Competition* organized by the Nepal Academy. He has 8 published books of poems and 7 published volumes of essays and travel essays. His works have been translated into English, Japanese, Korean, Hindi, Serbian, Slovenian and Tamil and have been appeared various national and international anthologies, Journals and magazines. He lives in Kathmandu with his family.

Sylvia Riojas Vaughn is a Pushcart Prize and Best of the Net nominee. Her work appears in *Red River Review, Triadæ, HOUSEBOAT,* and *Diálogo.*

Lita Verella began writing poetry in the eighth grade. Being known as the shy and quiet girl, her English Literature teacher took notice of what she had written, and how she would come alive when it came to studying and writing poetry. It was there where her teacher would encourage her to keep writing.

Her poetry has been featured in several anthologies and blogs, and she is currently working on her first poetry book to be titled, *The Beauty In Between.*

Marion de Vos is an American poet with 4 published collections amongst her several poems published in anthologies and magazines.

John Ward is a 63-year-old writer from the North of England. In 2015, he completed a BA (Open) with the Open University with a focus on creative writing. Much of his poetry and prose is personal, reflecting a life where love and loss have had a profound effect on his outpourings.

Robert West's third chapbook of poems, *Convalescent,* appeared from Finishing Line Press in 2011. He teaches at Mississippi State University.

Heidi Willson lives an hour from the West of Chicago, where she teaches French at Jefferson High School. Heidi enjoys writing, walking in nature, and learning about other cultures in free time. Her works have been published in the *Greek Fire* anthology and the *And The Tail Wagged On… anthology* as well as the *Shout it Out*! anthology by Lost Tower Publications

Abigail Elizabeth Ottley Wyatt was born in Aveley, Essex in 1952, but now lives in Penzance in Cornwall. Although she mainly writes poetry and short fiction she is now beginning to write for the stage. Over a ten-year period, her work has appeared in more than a hundred magazines, journals and anthologies including *Wave Hub: new poetry from Cornwall* (Francis Boutle). *Duet Mainly in Blues and Greys* is her ten-minute play; its debut performance took place at the St Ives Arts Club in May, 2016.